United States Government Accountability Office

Report to Congressional Committees

I0454868

April 2010

ENVIRONMENTAL SATELLITES

Strategy Needed to Sustain Critical Climate and Space Weather Measurements

GAO-10-456

April 2010

Highlights of GAO-10-456, a report to congressional committees

ENVIRONMENTAL SATELLITES

Strategy Needed to Sustain Critical Climate and Space Weather Measurements

Why GAO Did This Study

Environmental satellites provide data on the earth and its space environment that are used for forecasting the weather, measuring variations in climate over time, and predicting space weather. In planning for the next generation of these satellites, federal agencies originally sought to fulfill weather, climate, and space weather requirements. However, in 2006, federal agencies restructured two key satellite acquisitions, the National Polar-orbiting Operational Environmental Satellite System (NPOESS) and the Geostationary Operational Environmental Satellite-R series (GOES-R). This involved removing key climate and space weather instruments.

GAO was asked to (1) assess plans for restoring the capabilities that were removed from the two key satellite acquisitions, (2) evaluate federal efforts to establish a strategy for the long-term provision of satellite-provided climate data, and (3) evaluate federal efforts to establish a strategy for the long-term provision of satellite-provided space weather data. To do so, GAO analyzed agency plans and reports.

What GAO Recommends

GAO is making recommendations to the President's Assistant for Science and Technology to establish and implement interagency strategies for the long-term provision of environmental observations. The Assistant's office neither agreed nor disagreed with the recommendations, but noted its plan to develop a strategy for earth observations.

View GAO-10-456 or key components. For more information, contact David A. Powner at (202) 512-9286 or pownerd@gao.gov.

What GAO Found

After key climate and space weather instruments were removed from the NPOESS and GOES-R programs in 2006, federal agencies decided to restore selected capabilities in the near term. However, neither the National Oceanic and Atmospheric Administration (NOAA) nor the Department of Defense (DOD) has established plans to restore the full set of NPOESS capabilities over the life of the program. Further, NOAA has not made any plans to restore the advanced climate capabilities of the instrument that was removed from GOES-R. Expected gaps in coverage for the instruments that were removed range from 1 to 11 years, and begin as soon as 2015. Until these capabilities are in place, the agencies will not be able to provide key environmental data that are important for sustaining climate and space weather measurements.

For over a decade, federal agencies and the climate community have clamored for a national interagency strategy to coordinate agency priorities, budgets, and schedules for environmental satellite observations over the long-term— and the governance structure to implement that strategy. In mid-2009, a White House-sponsored interagency working group drafted a report that identifies and prioritizes near-term opportunities for environmental observations; however, the plan has not been approved by key entities within the Executive Office of the President and there is no schedule for finalizing it. In addition, the report does not address costs, schedules, or the long-term provision of satellite data, and there is no process or time frame for implementing it. Without a strategy for continuing environmental measurements over the coming decades and a means for implementing it, agencies will continue to independently pursue their immediate priorities on an ad hoc basis, the economic benefits of a coordinated approach to investments in earth observation may be lost, and our nation's ability to understand climate change may be limited.

While federal agencies have taken steps to plan for continued space weather observations in the near-term, they lack a strategy for the long-term provision of space weather data. NOAA and DOD plan to replace aging satellites, and an interagency space weather program drafted two reports on how to mitigate the loss of key satellites and instruments. These reports were submitted to the Executive Office of the President's Office of Science and Technology Policy (OSTP) in the fall of 2009. However, OSTP has no schedule for approving or releasing the reports. Until OSTP approves and releases the reports, it will not be clear whether the reports provide a strategy to ensure the long-term provision of space weather data—or whether the current efforts are simply attempts to ensure short-term data continuity. Without a comprehensive long-term strategy for the provision of space weather data, agencies may make ad hoc decisions to ensure continuity in the near term and risk making inefficient investment decisions.

Contents

Tables

Figures

Abbreviations

DOD	Department of Defense
DMSP	Defense Meteorological Satellite Program
GOES-R	Geostationary Operational Environmental Satellite System-R series
GPS	Global Positioning System
JPSS	Joint Polar Satellite System
MetOp	Meteorological Operational (satellite)
NASA	National Aeronautics and Space Administration
NOAA	National Oceanic and Atmospheric Administration
NPOESS	National Polar-orbiting Operational Environmental Satellite System
NPP	NPOESS Preparatory Project
OMB	Office of Management and Budget
OSTP	Office of Science and Technology Policy
POES	Polar Operational Environmental Satellites
USGEO	U.S. Group on Earth Observations
USGCRP	U.S. Global Change Research Program

GAO
Accountability * Integrity * Reliability

United States Government Accountability Office
Washington, DC 20548

April 27, 2010

The Honorable Brian Baird
Chairman
The Honorable Bob Inglis
Ranking Member
Subcommittee on Energy and Environment
Committee on Science and Technology
House of Representatives

The Honorable Brad Miller
Chairman
The Honorable Paul Broun, Jr.
Ranking Member
Subcommittee on Investigations and Oversight
Committee on Science and Technology
House of Representatives

Environment-observing satellites provide data that are used for weather forecasting, as well as climate monitoring, prediction, and research. Current satellites provide measurements of the earth's atmosphere, oceans, land, and space environment. For example, satellites provide data on precipitation, cloud cover, sea surface temperatures, land vegetation, snow cover, and solar flares. These data are used to provide warnings of severe storms and hurricanes, and to monitor and predict seasonal, annual, and decade-long changes in the earth's temperature and ozone coverage. They are also used to observe and forecast space weather, which is when solar activities such as solar flares and solar winds are expected to affect space and earth assets (including satellites, airplanes flying at high altitudes, and the electric power grid).

In planning for the next generation of environmental satellites to help observe and predict weather and climate, federal agencies originally established plans for polar and geostationary satellites that would meet a wide variety of missions. Specifically, the National Polar-orbiting Operational Environmental Satellite System (NPOESS) program—managed by the National Oceanic and Atmospheric Administration (NOAA), the National Aeronautics and Space Administration (NASA), and the Department of Defense (DOD)—was originally envisioned to fulfill requirements for global observations of weather, space weather, and climate.[1] In addition, NOAA's Geostationary Operational Environmental Satellite-R series (GOES-R) program was originally envisioned to fulfill requirements for continuous observations of weather, climate, and space weather for the continental United States and adjacent oceans. However, both of these programs were restructured due to growing costs. These restructuring efforts involved removing selected climate and space weather instruments and reducing the capabilities of other instruments. As a result, the United States' ability to sustain important climate and space weather measurements over the long term was put at risk.

This report responds to your request that we (1) assess plans for restoring the capabilities that were removed from the NPOESS and GOES-R satellites, (2) evaluate the adequacy of federal efforts to establish a strategy for the long-term provision of satellite-provided *climate* data, and (3) evaluate the adequacy of federal efforts to establish a strategy for the long-term provision of satellite-provided *space weather* data. To assess plans for restoring the capabilities that were removed from the NPOESS and GOES-R programs, we compared the original program plans for sensors and products with current plans for these and other satellite programs and identified gaps over time. To evaluate the adequacy of federal efforts to establish a strategy for the long-term provision of satellite-provided climate data, we compared plans for the provision of climate data with leading practices and past recommendations for the development of a long-term strategy, and we identified the shortfalls of and challenges to those plans. To evaluate the adequacy of federal efforts to establish a strategy for the long-term provision of satellite-provided space weather data, we compared plans for the provision of space weather data with leading practices for the development of a long-term strategy, and we identified the shortfalls of and challenges to those plans. We also visited key weather, space weather, and climate facilities to obtain information related to federal strategic planning efforts for space-based observations and interviewed relevant agency officials. In addition, this

---

[1]During our review, the White House announced plans to restructure the NPOESS program so that NOAA and DOD would no longer continue to jointly procure the satellite system. The NOAA portion of this restructured program is called the Joint Polar Satellite System (JPSS). However, detailed plans about what the restructuring entails and when it will occur have not yet been established. Thus, in this report, we will continue to refer to this program as the NPOESS program.

report builds on work we have done on environmental satellites and climate change over the last several years.[2]

We conducted this performance audit from June 2009 to April 2010, in accordance with generally accepted government auditing standards. Those standards require that we plan and perform the audit to obtain sufficient, appropriate evidence to provide a reasonable basis for our findings and conclusions based on our audit objectives. We believe that the evidence obtained provides a reasonable basis for our findings and conclusions based on our audit objectives. Additional details on our objectives, scope, and methodology are provided in appendix I.

Background

Since the 1960s, the United States has used satellites to observe the earth and its land, oceans, atmosphere, and space environments. Satellites provide a global perspective of the environment and allow observations in areas that may be otherwise unreachable or unsuitable for measurements. Used in combination with ground, sea, and airborne observing systems,

---

[2]GAO, *Climate Change Adaptation: Strategic Federal Planning Could Help Government Officials Make More Informed Decisions*, GAO-10-113 (Washington, D.C.: Oct. 7, 2009); *Polar-orbiting Environmental Satellites: With Costs Increasing and Data Continuity at Risk, Improvements Needed in Tri-Agency Decision Making*, GAO-09-564 (Washington, D.C.: June 17, 2009); *Geostationary Operational Environmental Satellites: Acquisition is Under Way but Improvements Needed in Management and Oversight*, GAO-09-323 (Washington, D.C.: Apr. 2, 2009); *Environmental Satellites: Polar-orbiting Satellite Acquisition Faces Delays, Decisions Needed on Whether and How to Ensure Climate Data Continuity*, GAO-08-899T (Washington, D.C.: June 19, 2008); *Environmental Satellites: Polar-orbiting Satellite Acquisition Faces Delays; Decisions Needed on Whether and How to Ensure Climate Data Continuity*, GAO-08-518 (Washington, D.C.: May 16, 2008); *Geostationary Operational Environmental Satellites: Progress Has Been Made, but Improvements Are Needed to Effectively Manage Risks*, GAO-08-18 (Washington, D.C.: Oct. 23, 2007); *Environmental Satellite Acquisitions: Progress and Challenges*; GAO-07-1099T (Washington, D.C.: July 11, 2007); *Polar-orbiting Operational Environmental Satellites: Restructuring Is Under Way, but Challenges and Risks Remain*, GAO-07-910T (Washington, D.C.: June 7, 2007); *Polar-orbiting Operational Environmental Satellites: Restructuring Is Under Way, but Technical Challenges and Risks Remain*, GAO-07-498 (Washington, D.C.: Apr. 27, 2007); *Polar-orbiting Operational Environmental Satellites: Cost Increases Trigger Review and Place Program's Direction on Hold*, GAO-06-573T (Washington, D.C.: Mar. 30, 2006); *Geostationary Operational Environmental Satellites: Additional Action Needed to Incorporate Lessons Learned from Other Satellite Programs*, GAO-06-1129T (Washington, D.C.: Sept. 29, 2006); *Geostationary Operational Environmental Satellites: Steps Remain in Incorporating Lessons Learned from Other Satellite Programs*, GAO-06-993 (Washington, D.C.: Sept. 6, 2006); and *Polar-orbiting Operational Environmental Satellites: Technical Problems, Cost Increases, and Schedule Delays Trigger Need for Difficult Trade-off Decisions*, GAO-06-249T (Washington, D.C.: Nov. 16, 2005).

satellites have become an indispensable part of measuring and forecasting weather and climate. For example, satellites provide the graphical images used to identify current weather patterns, as well as the data that go into numerical weather prediction models. These models are used to forecast weather 1 to 2 weeks in advance and to issue warnings about severe weather, including the path and intensity of hurricanes. Satellite data are also used to warn infrastructure owners when increased solar activity is expected to affect key assets, including communication satellites or the electric power grid. When collected over time, satellite data can also be used to observe trends and changes in the earth's climate. For example, these data are used to monitor and project seasonal, annual, and decadal changes in the earth's temperature, vegetation coverage, and ozone coverage.

Current Environmental Satellite Programs Include Both Operational and Research Satellites

Environmental satellite programs generally fall into two categories: operational satellites and research and development satellites. Operational environmental satellites contribute to weather and climate predictions on a regular basis, and federal agencies sustain them by launching new satellites as older ones reach the end of their useful lives. Alternatively, research and development satellites are designed to test new technologies or to provide insights into environmental science. While there is not a commitment to sustain the capabilities demonstrated on research and development satellites on subsequent missions, these capabilities can be included on operational satellites if they demonstrate the usefulness of a new measurement or the maturity of new technology. Currently, the United States operates a fleet of operational environmental satellites, as well as multiple research and development satellites.

Operational Environmental Satellites

Operational environmental satellites conduct earth observations from space in either a low-earth polar orbit or a geostationary earth orbit. Polar-orbiting satellites circle the earth in an almost north-south orbit within 1,250 miles of the earth, providing global coverage of conditions that affect weather and climate. Each satellite makes about 14 orbits a day. As the earth rotates beneath it, each satellite views the entire earth's surface twice a day. In contrast, geostationary satellites maintain a fixed position relative to the earth from an orbit of about 22,300 miles in space. Figure 1 describes key characteristics of polar-orbiting and geostationary satellites.

Figure 1: Characteristics of Polar and Geostationary Satellites

Polar satellites
- Low earth orbit (less than 1,250 miles above the earth)
- Take approximately 90-120 minutes to orbit the earth
- Travel in a North-South direction

Geostationary satellites
- At least 22,300 miles above the earth
- Take approximately 24 hours to orbit the earth, keeping them in a fixed position relative to the earth's surface

Sun

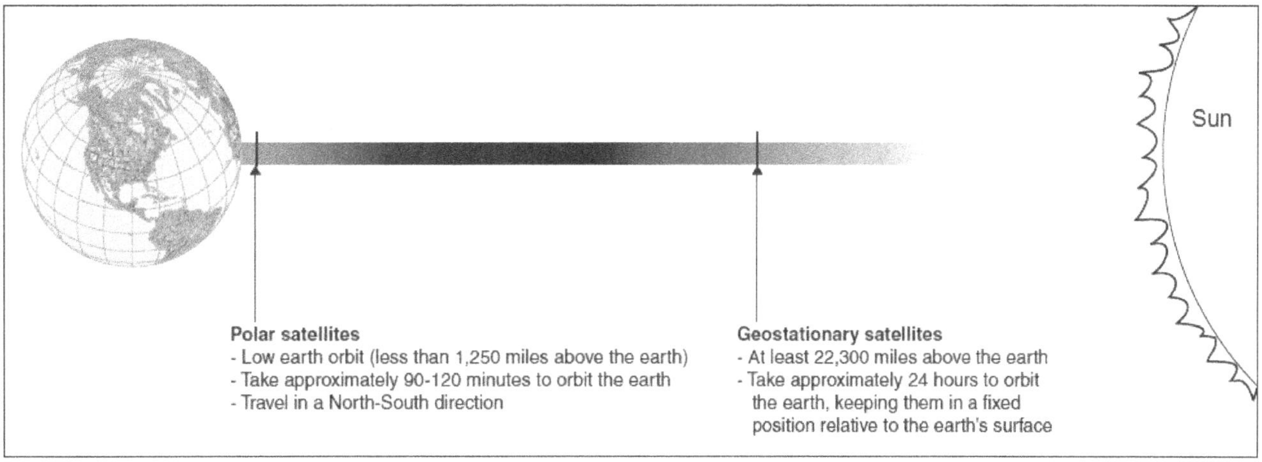

Sources: GAO and MapArt.

The United States currently operates two operational polar-orbiting meteorological satellite systems: the Polar Operational Environmental Satellites (POES) series, which is managed by NOAA, and the Defense Meteorological Satellite Program (DMSP), which is managed by the Air Force. The POES and DMSP programs provide data that are processed to provide graphical weather images and specialized weather products. They also provide the predominant input into numerical weather prediction models, a primary tool for forecasting weather. These satellites also provide data used to monitor environmental phenomena, such as ozone depletion, drought conditions, and energetic particle activity in the near-earth space environment, as well as data sets that are used by researchers to monitor climate change.

Currently, one POES and two DMSP satellites are positioned so that they can observe the earth in early morning, midmorning, and early afternoon polar orbits. In addition, a European satellite, called the Meteorological Operational (MetOp) satellite, provides observations in the midmorning orbit.[3] Together, they ensure that, for any region of the earth, the data

---

[3]The European Organisation for the Exploitation of Meteorological Satellites' MetOp program is a series of three polar-orbiting satellites dedicated to operational meteorology. The first of the MetOp satellites was launched in 2006; others are planned to be launched sequentially over 14 years.

provided to users are generally no more than 6 hours old. Figure 2 illustrates the current operational polar satellite configuration.

Figure 2: Configuration of Operational Polar Satellites

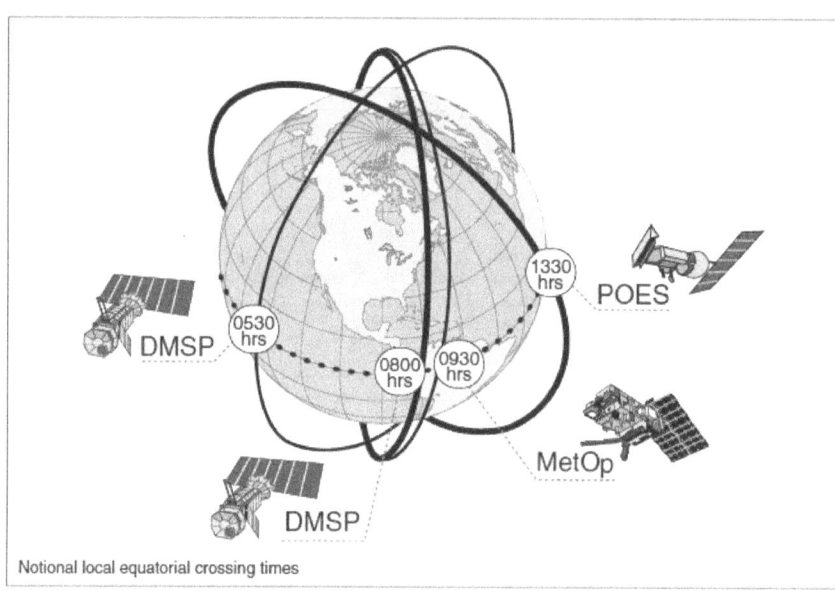

Notional local equatorial crossing times

Sources: GAO analysis of NPOESS and DOD data; MapArt (globe).

NOAA, NASA, and DOD are currently developing the next generation of operational polar-orbiting environmental satellites, called NPOESS. This program was planned to converge the POES and DMSP satellite programs into a single program capable of satisfying both civilian and military requirements for earth and space weather, as well as climate monitoring. As currently defined, NPOESS consists of a series of four satellites, as well as a demonstration satellite called the NPOESS Preparatory Project (NPP). NPP is intended to reduce the risk associated with launching new sensor technologies and to ensure continuity of climate data. The agencies plan to launch NPP in 2011, with the other satellites following at regular intervals to ensure satellite coverage in two orbits through 2026. Due to poor program performance and interagency conflicts over system requirements, the NPOESS program is currently being restructured to allow separate acquisitions by NOAA and DOD. However, it is not yet clear how or when this transition will take place.

In addition to the polar satellite program, NOAA also manages an operational geostationary satellite program, called the Geostationary Operational Environmental Satellite (GOES) program. NOAA operates GOES as a two-satellite system that is primarily focused on the United States (see fig. 3). These satellites are uniquely positioned to provide broad, continuously updated coverage of atmospheric and surface conditions on the earth, as well as the space environment surrounding the earth. For example, geostationary satellites observe the development of hazardous weather events, such as hurricanes and severe thunderstorms, and track their movement and intensity to help reduce or avoid major losses of property and life. In addition, the geostationary satellites track space weather variables such as solar X-ray fluctuations and high-energy particles that are used in identifying emerging solar storms.

Figure 3: Approximate GOES Geographic Coverage

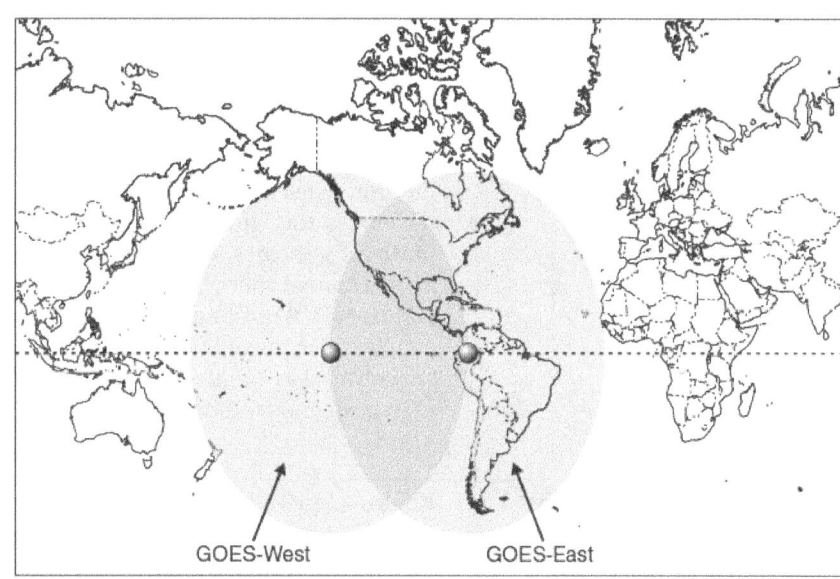

GOES-West   GOES-East

Sources: NOAA (data); MapArt (map).

NOAA is currently developing the next generation geostationary series, called GOES-R. GOES-R is expected to provide satellite data products to users more quickly and to provide better clarity and precision than prior geostationary satellites. It is expected to be a two-satellite system, launching in 2015 and 2017, and is considered critical to the United States' ability to maintain the continuity of data required for weather forecasting through 2028.

Research Satellites	In addition to operational polar and geostationary satellites, the United States operates research satellites to better understand scientific earth processes and to develop new technologies. Since the early 1990s, NASA has launched 18 research satellites under its Earth Observing System, and plans to launch 6 more by 2013.[4] These satellites continue to provide global and seasonal earth system measurements, which have provided a better understanding of human impacts on the earth, as well as improved disaster prediction and mitigation technologies. They are used both by NASA's research communities and by other agencies, including the U.S. Department of Agriculture, for operational and decision-making purposes. NASA is now planning the next generation of research satellites, called its Earth Systematic Missions program. This program consists of three series of satellites to advance understanding of the climate system and climate change. In addition to its earth observation activities, NASA has been working to understand and measure solar activity in the space environment. For example, the observations of solar winds from its Advanced Composition Explorer mission and solar X-ray images from its Solar and Heliospheric Observatory mission are used for both solar research and space weather forecasting.
	DOD also develops environmental research satellites in support of its mission when a need is identified. For example, the Navy and others developed the WindSat program to demonstrate new capabilities for measuring the ocean surface wind vectors from space and to demonstrate an instrument that was originally planned for the NPOESS mission. In addition, DOD's Communication/Navigation Outage Forecasting System satellite is expected to develop a capability for detecting and forecasting space weather events that lead to disruptions in communication signals in high-frequency radios and Global Positioning System (GPS) satellites.
Environmental Satellite Data and Products	Environmental satellites gather a broad range of data that are transformed into a variety of products. Satellite sensors observe different bands of radiation wavelengths, called channels, which are used for remotely

---

[4]NASA's Earth Observing System program consists of 24 coordinated polar-orbiting satellites designed to monitor and understand key components of the climate system and their interactions through long-term global observations. Many of these missions also have international partners. Key satellites within the Earth Observing System include the Aura satellite, which focuses on atmospheric chemistry and composition; the Aqua satellite, which focuses on the earth's water cycle, atmosphere, and land; and the Terra satellite, which focuses on land, oceans, and atmosphere.

determining information about the earth's environment. When first received, satellite data are considered raw data. To make them usable, NOAA, NASA, and DOD operate data processing centers that format the data so that they are time-sequenced and include earth location and calibration information. After formatting, these data are called raw data records. The data centers further process the raw data records into channel-specific data sets, called sensor data records and temperature data records. These data records are then used to derive weather and climate products called environmental data records and climate data records.

Environmental data records generally support near-term weather observations and include a wide range of atmospheric products detailing cloud coverage, temperature, humidity, and ozone distribution; land surface products showing snow cover, vegetation, and land use; ocean products depicting sea surface temperatures, sea ice, and wave height; and characterizations of the space environment. Combinations of these data records (raw, sensor, temperature, and environmental data records) are also used to derive more sophisticated products, including the forecasts that result from weather prediction modeling. In contrast, climate data records identify longer term variations in the climate and include observations of the land, ocean, and atmosphere.

While environmental and climate data products use much of the same data, the two user communities' needs differ. In order to deliver timely weather forecasts and warnings, meteorologists require the rapid delivery of environmental data. Alternatively, scientists involved in climate monitoring, prediction, and research require accurate, precise, and consistent data over long periods of time. Figure 4 is a simplified depiction of the various stages of environmental satellite data processing, and figure 5 depicts examples of two different weather products. Figure 6 depicts an example of a climate data record.

Figure 4: Stages of Satellite Data Processing

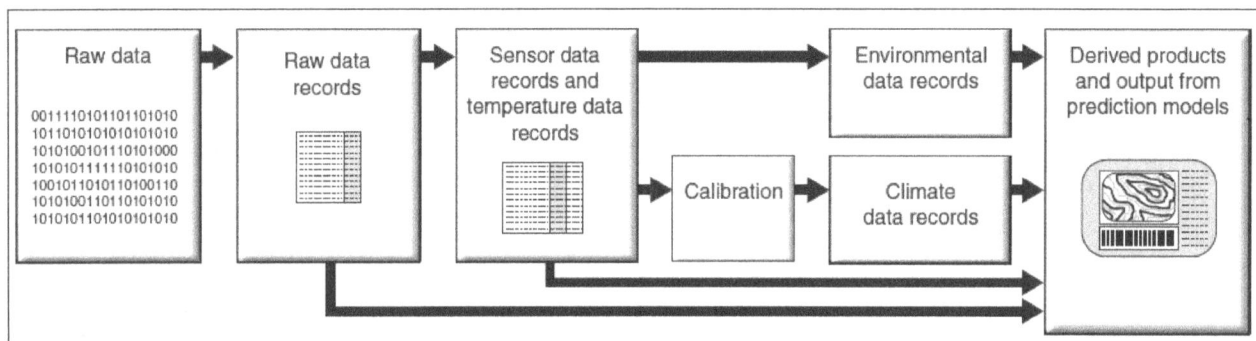

Sources: GAO analysis of NASA and NOAA information.

Figure 5: Examples of Weather Products

Source: NOAA's National Environmental Satellite Data and Information Service.

Note: The figure on the left is a POES Image of Hurricane Katrina in 2005, and the figure on the right is an analysis of ozone concentration produced from POES satellite data.

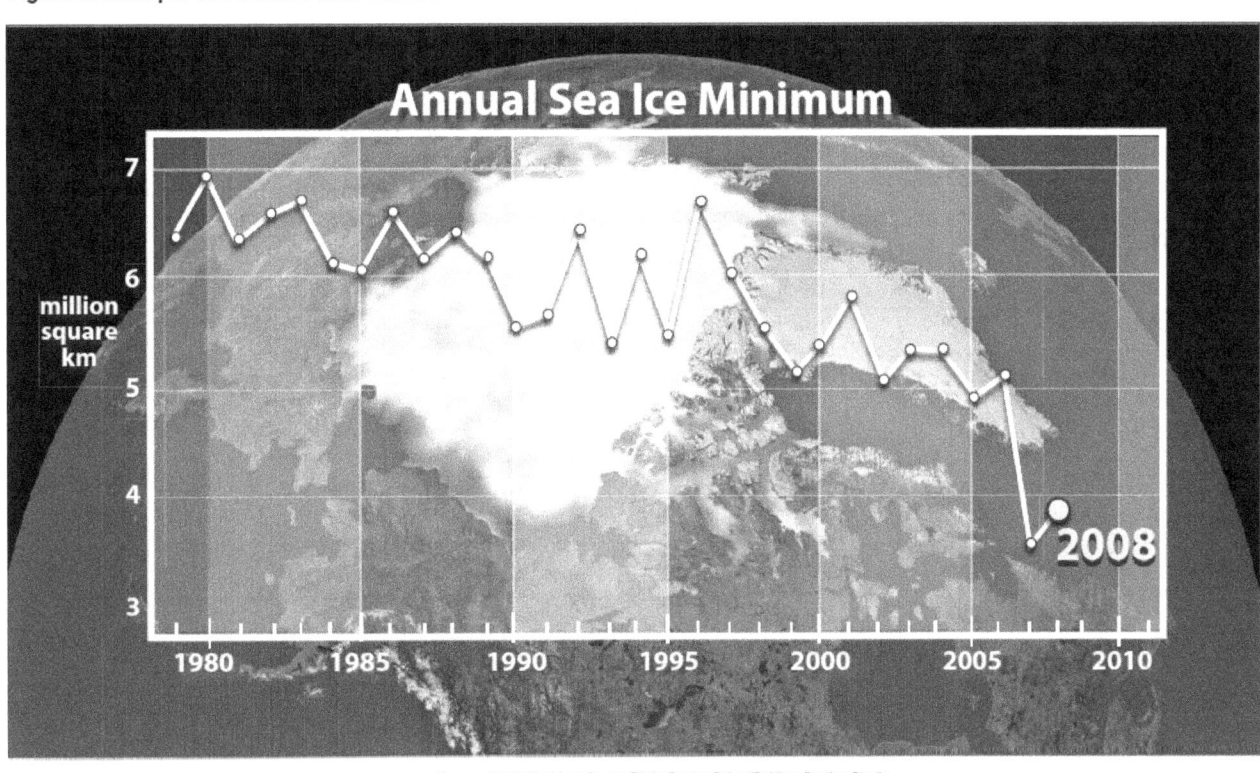

Source: NASA/Goddard Space Flight Center Scientific Visualization Studio.

Note: This image depicts the minimum sea ice concentration (the fewest number of square kilometers (km) of Arctic area covered with sea ice) in successive Septembers from 1979-2008. The data was collected by the Special Sensor Microwave/Imager sensor on DOD's DMSP satellites.

An Overview of Climate Products and Uses

One subset of satellite-provided environmental weather information is climate data. Satellite-provided climate data are used in combination with ground and ocean observing systems to understand seasonal, annual, and decadal variations in the climate. Satellites provide land observations such as measurements of soil moisture, changes in how land is used, and vegetation growth; ocean observations such as sea levels, sea surface temperature, and ocean color; and atmospheric observations such as greenhouse gas levels (e.g., carbon dioxide), aerosol and dust particles, and moisture concentration. When these data are obtained over long periods of time, scientists are able to use them to determine short- and long-term trends in how the earth's systems work and how they work together. For example, climate measurements have allowed scientists to better understand the effect of deforestation on how the earth absorbs heat, retains rainwater, and absorbs greenhouse gases. Scientists also use climate data to help predict climate cycles that affect the weather, such as El Niño, and to develop global estimates of food crop production for a particular year or season. Table 1 provides examples of ways in which satellite-provided climate products are used.

Table 1: Examples of Satellite-Provided Climate Products and Their Uses

Products	Uses
Precipitation analysis Assesses the probability for accumulation of precipitation (rainfall or snowfall) or changes from normal precipitation amounts for given regions.	• Agricultural industry uses for decisions such as crop mixture, crop insurance needs, and timing and amount of irrigation needed. • Water managers use for plans in developing and operating water reservoirs, as well as predicting river flow. • Health officials use for studies of impacts to human health (e.g., malaria, cholera, and other water-borne diseases).
Land cover/vegetation and land use analysis Assesses the location, health, and types of plant life for given regions and areas of land that can be developed for urbanization or other land uses.	• Scientists and wildlife conservation managers use in studying the impacts of changes in land cover/vegetation on wildlife (e.g., loss of food source, habitat). • Forestry managers use for decisions on when and where to restrict burning in order to prevent wildfire outbreaks. • Transportation officials use in determining placement of highways and train routes. • Agricultural industry and humanitarian assistance planners use crop coverage to help predict world food supply and shortages. • Scientists and land use planners use to determine how certain areas will respond to changing weather, as well as to better understand global changes in greenhouse gases and the earth's heat retention.
Sea wave and wind analysis Assesses wave heights and wind conditions over the ocean to describe sea states and potentially adverse tropical weather.	• Marine cargo industry uses for routing and scheduling shipping routes. • U.S. Navy uses for military logistics and planning. • Petroleum industry uses in offshore drilling operations.
Sea ice analysis Assesses the location of ice and changes in ice characteristics.	• Marine cargo industry uses to identify available or emerging shipping routes. • U.S. Navy uses in Arctic sea ice models for long-range planning for fleet operations.
Land surface temperature analysis Assesses the probability for surface temperature ranges and deviations from normal temperatures for given regions.	• Health officials use in identifying potentially adverse health affects on humans (e.g., heat stress, disease outbreaks such as malaria and avian influenza). • Producers and consumers of natural gas and electricity use to identify changing energy demand based on changes in temperatures.
Cloud physics and aerosol analysis Assesses the presence of clouds, smoke, and dust and their impacts to satellite or aircraft instruments.	• The U.S. Air Force uses for military airborne planning and operations. • Climate scientists use to account for the effects that cloud properties may have on other satellite-based observations.

Products	Uses
Severe weather seasonal outlooks	• Insurance industry uses in identifying potential liabilities and risk of losses.
Assesses the probability of the number and severity of severe weather events such as hurricanes, floods, and tornadoes.	• The Federal Emergency Management Agency uses for emergency preparedness and response activities. • Weather forecasters use to help analyze the likelihood of certain weather events such as hurricanes.

Sources: GAO analysis of data from DOD, NASA, NOAA, the U.S. Group on Earth Observations (USGEO), the U.S. Global Change Research Program (USGCRP), and the National Research Council.

An Overview of Space Weather Products and Uses

Another subset of satellite-provided environmental weather information is space weather. Satellite-provided observations of space weather generally describe changes in solar activity in the space environment. Just as scientists use observations of weather that occurs on the earth's surface and in its atmosphere to develop forecasts, scientists and researchers use space weather observations to detect and forecast solar storms that may be potentially harmful to society. Examples of space weather observations include bursts of solar energy called solar flares, solar winds, geomagnetic activity associated with solar storms, solar X-ray images and fluctuations, and solar ultraviolet images and fluctuations. These activities can adversely impact space assets (such as communication, GPS, and environmental satellites), airplanes flying at high altitudes or over the poles, ground assets (such as the electric energy grid), and the communications infrastructure (including high-frequency radio communications and transmissions between GPS satellites and ground-based receivers). Figure 7 provides an illustration of the key assets that are affected by solar weather and the solar weather activities that could put these assets at risk, while table 2 provides examples of ways in which space weather products and services are used.

Figure 7: Key Assets and Risks in the Earth's Space Environment

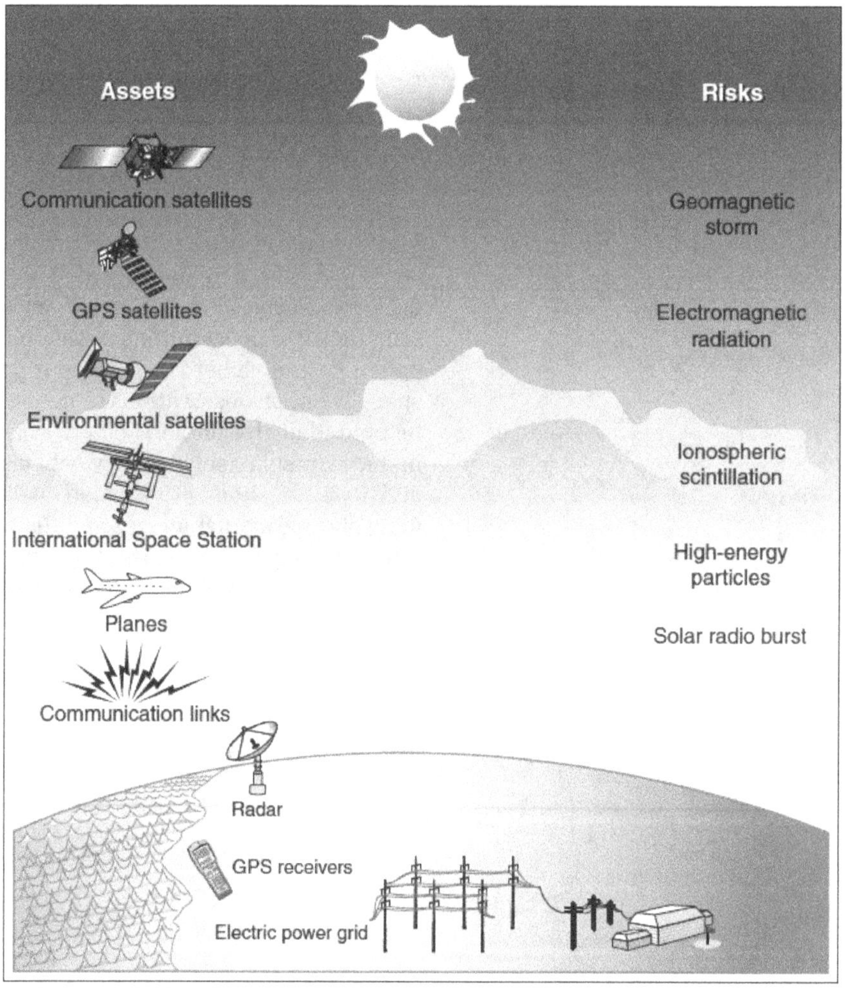

Source: GAO.

GAO-10-456 Environmental Satellites

Table 2: Examples of Satellite-Provided Space Weather Products and Their Uses

Products	Uses
Energetic particle analysis Assesses the occurrence of energetic electrons, protons, and heavy ions in space.	• Satellite operators use to protect satellite components from damage and to correct for satellite disorientation. • NASA space mission control managers use to assess potential damage to spacecraft and potential harm to astronauts. • The Federal Aviation Administration uses to assess potential radiation hazards to passengers during high-altitude flights.
Ionospheric disturbance analysis Assesses how solar activity disturbs the dynamic environment within the upper atmosphere.	• Military forces monitor for potential disruption to the Global Positioning System, which can affect military positioning, navigation, and timing of military operations. • Others interested in using GPS for land and sea-based navigation monitor for potential errors.
Solar X-rays and radio burst analysis Assesses bursts of solar radio waves and X-rays emitted from the sun.	• Satellite operators use to correct satellite orbital drift and geolocation errors. • The military uses to monitor potential radar interference, satellite communication interference, and high-frequency radio blackouts.
Solar wind analysis Assesses the path, severity, and timing of space weather events that are approaching the earth's space environment.	• Civilian and military space weather forecasters use to send out space weather warnings, watches, and alerts. • NASA researchers use to investigate the sun and its effects on the earth and solar system.
Geomagnetic storm analysis Assesses solar activity that causes disturbances of the earth's magnetic field.	• The military uses to assess potential launch trajectory errors and radar interference. • Electric power grid managers monitor for potential damage to or failure of the power grid.

Sources: GAO analysis of DOD, NOAA, and National Research Council data.

Federal Responsibilities for Environmental Satellites, Satellite Data Processing, and Climate and Space Weather Products

Three key federal agencies—NOAA, NASA, and DOD—are responsible for managing environmental satellite programs, processing the collected environmental data into usable climate and space weather products and services, and disseminating the data and products to others. Many other agencies use these data and products to support their missions. For example, the Department of Agriculture uses temperature, precipitation, and soil moisture data and products to inform farmers on what to plant, when to plant, and strategies to employ during the growing season, while the Department of Energy uses space weather information to help determine when the electrical grid could be damaged by solar events. These agencies also participate in one or more federal working groups that coordinate the agencies' needs for and uses of environmental satellite products. These interagency working groups are overseen by offices within the Executive Office of the President.

| Climate Responsibilities | NOAA, DOD, and NASA manage multiple organizations with a diverse set of climate responsibilities. Specifically, NOAA has several organizations with responsibilities for developing and using satellite data to monitor and predict the earth's climate.[5] These include the following: |

- The National Environmental Satellite, Data, and Information Service manages the development of environmental satellite products. It also has three data centers that archive environmental data and products related to climate, oceans, and geophysical features and disseminate these data and products to the public.

- The National Weather Service is responsible for weather, hydrologic, and climate forecasts and advisories for the United States, its territories, and adjacent waters and ocean areas for the protection of life and property and the enhancement of the national economy. Through its National Centers for Environmental Prediction's Climate Prediction Center, it disseminates products and services that describe the earth's climate and provides near-term climate predictions.

- The Office of Oceanic and Atmospheric Research has climate responsibilities focusing on understanding causes of global climate change and on improving operational climate forecasting capabilities through its Earth System Research Laboratory and Geophysical Fluid Dynamics Laboratory.

Organizations within DOD also have responsibilities for providing climate forecasts that are specifically tailored for military planning and operations. For example, the Air Force Weather Agency is responsible for providing environmental outlooks to support the Air Force and Army, including forecasts of the properties of clouds (such as density or ice content) and ground conditions to support planning for airborne and ground operations. In addition, the Navy's Naval Oceanographic Office tracks ocean currents for planning ship tracking and missions, and provides outlooks of the acoustical environment for submarines. The Navy's Fleet Numerical Meteorology and Oceanography Command provides environmental outlooks in support of naval operations, including outlooks on coastal and open ocean conditions.

---

[5]In February 2010, NOAA announced that it would create a NOAA Climate Service. However, it is not yet clear what the service's responsibilities will include.

NASA's Earth Science Division is responsible for advancing the understanding of the earth system and demonstrating new satellite technologies through its environmental research and development satellites. NASA currently demonstrates new measurements and technologies for measuring climate through various satellite and airborne missions, including the Earth Observing System.

In addition to NOAA, DOD, and NASA, the Department of the Interior's U.S. Geological Survey is responsible for operating the Landsat satellites, distributing the data, and maintaining an archive of Landsat 7 and other remotely sensed data.

Other agencies use climate products in their operations. For example, the Environmental Protection Agency uses sea level data and products to examine the potential societal impacts, adaptation options, and other decisions sensitive to sea level rise in coastal communities, while the Department of Homeland Security's Federal Emergency Management Agency uses climate research and predictions to help develop disaster preparedness and response plans. Additional processing and product development is done in partnership with universities, nongovernmental organizations, and industry. See appendix II for more information on federal agencies and their climate-related responsibilities.

Space Weather Responsibilities

NOAA, DOD, and NASA also manage organizations with responsibilities for space weather satellites and prediction. NOAA and DOD both obtain satellite and land-based measurements of solar activity and produce operational space weather products for a variety of users. Specifically, NOAA's National Weather Service manages the Space Weather Prediction Center, which is responsible for continuously monitoring space weather for civilian user communities, and provides official space weather warnings, watches, and alerts.[6] In addition, NOAA's National Environmental Satellite, Data, and Information Service has a data center that archives environmental data related to space weather and disseminates them to the public.

Complementing NOAA's responsibilities for civilian space weather forecasts, DOD's Air Force Weather Agency is responsible for

---

[6]According to agency officials, space weather warnings predict solar activities that are expected to have an impact within minutes to hours, while watches predict solar activities that are expected to have impact within 24 to 72 hours, and alerts indicate activity that has been observed or is currently ongoing.

continuously monitoring space weather for defense and intelligence user communities. The Air Force Weather Agency and NOAA products are similar, and the majority of the space weather data they use are the same. However, the Air Force customizes specialized products to provide space situational awareness for its users.[7] Both the Air Force and NOAA work together to ensure that both the civilian and military sectors understand and can respond to changes in the space environment.

NASA conducts space weather research and development activities using environmental satellites. For instance, NASA observes solar wind data from its Advanced Composition Explorer mission[8] and solar X-ray images from its Solar and Heliospheric Observatory mission to better understand the sun and its effects on the earth and solar system. Data from these satellites are used for solar research and are also used by other agencies for operational space weather forecasting, including watches and warnings.

Other federal agencies use space weather products to support their respective missions. For example, the Department of Transportation's Federal Aviation Administration examines radiation exposure at high altitudes, while the Department of Energy uses observations from space weather satellites to study possible impacts on electrical energy transmission through the energy grid. See appendix II for more information on federal agencies and their space-weather-related responsibilities.

Interagency Coordination of Satellite-Provided Environmental Observations

In addition to agencies with responsibilities for acquiring, processing and disseminating environmental data and information, there are two organizations—the U.S. Group on Earth Observations (USGEO) and the U.S. Global Change Research Program (USGCRP)—that are primarily responsible for coordinating federal efforts with respect to observations of the earth's environment. The National Space Weather Program serves as the coordinating body for space weather.

---

[7]Space situational awareness is an understanding of activity that is occurring in the space environment, including potential threats to space exploration and national defense readiness.

[8]The Advanced Composition Explorer is well beyond its design life and could fail at any time.

- USGEO is made up of representatives from federal agencies with a role in earth observations, as well as liaisons from the Executive Office of the President. The group's responsibilities include developing and coordinating an ongoing process for planning, developing, and managing an integrated U.S. earth-observing system consisting of ground, airborne, and satellite measurements.[9] USGEO reports to the National Science and Technology Council's Committee on Environment and Natural Resources.

- USGCRP consists of representatives from 13 federal departments and agencies, as well as liaisons from the Executive Office of the President and USGEO. Congress established USGCRP in 1990 to coordinate and integrate federal research on changes in the global environment and to discuss its implications for society. USGCRP reports to the National Science and Technology Council's Committee on Environment and Natural Resources.

- The National Space Weather Program is responsible for coordinating federal efforts and leveraging resources with respect to space weather observation. The program consists of representatives from eight federal agencies, who coordinate their activities through NOAA's Office of the Federal Coordinator for Meteorology.

Appendix III identifies the federal organizations that participate in these interagency coordination groups.

Executive Oversight of Federal Environmental Observations

The Executive Office of the President provides oversight for federal space based environmental observation. Within the Executive Office of the President, the Office of Science and Technology Policy (OSTP), the Office of Management and Budget (OMB), and the Council on Environmental Quality carry out these governance responsibilities. In addition, the National Science and Technology Council and its Committee on Environment and Natural Resources provide the Executive Office of the President with executive-level coordination and advice. Table 3 identifies roles and responsibilities of organizations within the Executive Office of

---

[9]USGEO also supports the Global Earth Observation System of Systems, an international effort to share environmental data to support decision-making in nine societal benefit areas: agriculture, biodiversity, climate, disasters, ecosystems, energy, health, water, and weather. According to its charter, the Global Earth Observation System of Systems is to provide the overall conceptual and organizational framework needed to move toward integrated global earth observations to meet user needs.

the President that provide oversight of federal environmental observation efforts.

Table 3: Organizations within the Executive Office of the President That Provide Oversight of Environmental Observations

Organization	Oversight responsibility
OSTP	OSTP is responsible for, among other things, providing scientific and technical analysis with respect to major policies, plans, and programs of the federal government; leading an interagency effort to develop and implement sound science and technology policies and budgets; and building partnerships among federal, state, and local governments, other countries, and the scientific community.
	The Assistant to the President for Science and Technology is also the Director of OSTP.
OMB	OMB is responsible for overseeing federal program budget planning; evaluating the effectiveness of agency programs, policies, and procedures; assessing competing funding demands among agencies; and setting funding priorities.
Council on Environmental Quality	The council coordinates federal environmental efforts and works with agencies and other White House offices in the development of environmental policies and initiatives.
National Science and Technology Council	This is a cabinet-level council that coordinates science and technological policies among federal research and development entities and sets national goals for science and technology investments.
	The council's Committee on Environment and Natural Resources provides advice on federal research and development efforts in the area of environment and natural resources.
	The Assistant to the President for Science and Technology functions as the head of the council and its committees, while OSTP provides administrative support.

Source: GAO analysis of Executive Office of the President responsibilities.

Prior GAO Reports Recommended Developing Plans to Restore Cancelled Instruments

In recent years, we have issued a series of reports on the NPOESS and GOES-R satellite programs.[10] Both programs are critical to United States' ability to maintain the continuity of data required for weather forecasting and global climate monitoring through the years 2026 and 2028, respectively. However, both of these programs were restructured due to their complexity and growing costs. These restructuring efforts involved removing selected climate and space weather instruments. Specifically, on the NPOESS program, four instruments were removed and four had their capabilities reduced. On the GOES-R program, NOAA removed an advanced instrument that was important to the weather and climate community. In May 2008, we recommended that the agencies develop a long-term strategy for restoring the NPOESS sensors in order to guide

---

[10]The most recent GAO reports include GAO-09-564, GAO-09-323, GAO-08-518, and GAO-08-18.

short-term decision making and to avoid an ad hoc approach to restoring capabilities.[11] In addition, in April 2009, we recommended that NOAA develop a plan for restoring the advanced GOES-R capabilities that were removed from the program, if feasible and justified.[12]

Federal Agencies Have Not Established Plans to Restore All Capabilities Removed from the NPOESS and GOES-R Programs

Federal agencies have not yet established plans to restore all of the capabilities removed from the NPOESS[13] and GOES-R programs. As originally planned, the NPOESS and GOES-R programs included instruments and products to meet a wide range of user needs through 2026 and 2028, respectively. Specifically, both NPOESS and GOES-R were envisioned to fulfill requirements for weather, space weather, and climate monitoring. However, in 2006, both of these programs were restructured due to growing costs. These restructuring efforts involved removing selected climate and space weather instruments—and, in some cases, replacing them with a less-capable instrument. Table 4 lists the instruments that were removed or degraded.

Table 4: Instruments and Products Removed from the NPOESS and GOES-R Programs

Satellite program	Instrument	Instrument description	Restructuring decision/status
NPOESS	Aerosol Polarimetry Sensor	Retrieves specific measurements of clouds and aerosols (liquid droplets or solid particles suspended in the atmosphere, such as sea spray, smog, and smoke).	This instrument was cancelled from the two afternoon satellites (C1 and C3). Two products (aerosol refractive index and cloud particle size and distribution) will no longer be produced.
NPOESS	Conical-Scanning Microwave Imager/Sounder	Collects microwave images and data needed to measure rain rate, ocean surface wind speed and direction, amount of water in the clouds, and soil moisture, as well as temperature and humidity at different atmospheric levels.	This instrument was cancelled from all four NPOESS satellites and is to be replaced by a less complex *Microwave Imager/Sounder* instrument on the second, third, and fourth NPOESS satellites. In combination with another instrument, the Microwave Imager/Sounder is expected to provide all of the products that were originally planned, except for a soil moisture product (which will be degraded).

---

[11]GAO-08-518.

[12]GAO-09-323.

[13]During our review, the White House announced plans to restructure the NPOESS program so that it would no longer be jointly procured. Because detailed plans for the NOAA portion (JPSS) and DOD portion have not been established, we focused on the NPOESS program.

Satellite program	Instrument	Instrument description	Restructuring decision/status
NPOESS	Earth Radiation Budget Sensor	Measures solar short-wave radiation and long-wave radiation released by the earth back into space on a worldwide scale to enhance long-term climate studies.	This instrument was cancelled from the two afternoon satellites (C1 and C3) and replaced by a legacy sensor (called the *Clouds and Earth's Radiant Energy System*) on the first satellite only. The legacy sensor is expected to provide all of the products that were originally planned.
NPOESS	Ozone Mapping and Profiler Suite (nadir/limb)	Collects data needed to measure the amount and distribution of ozone in the earth's atmosphere. Consists of two components (limb and nadir) that can be provided separately.	One part of this instrument (nadir) is to be included on NPP and on the first and third NPOESS satellites. The other part (limb) was canceled, but it will be included on NPP. Without the limb component, one product (ozone total column/profile) will be degraded.
NPOESS	Radar Altimeter	Measures variances in sea surface height/topography and ocean surface roughness, which are used to determine sea height, significant wave height, and ocean surface wind speed and to provide critical inputs to ocean forecasting and climate prediction models.	This instrument was cancelled from the two early morning satellites (C2 and C4). NOAA and the Navy are planning to procure separate altimetry satellites.
NPOESS	Space Environmental Sensor Suite	Collects data to identify, reduce, and predict the effects of space weather on technological systems, including satellites and radio links.	This sensor suite was cancelled from three NPOESS satellites (C2, C3, and C4) and replaced by a less capable and less expensive legacy sensor suite (called the *Space Environment Monitor*) on the first and third NPOESS satellites (C1 and C3). The legacy sensor will provide 5 of the 13 planned products. The 8 products that will no longer be produced include electric fields, geomagnetic fields and in situ plasma fluctuations.
NPOESS	Total Solar Irradiance Sensor	Monitors and captures total and spectral solar irradiance data.	This sensor was cancelled from the two early morning satellites (C2 and C4). NOAA plans to include a replacement sensor on the first NPOESS satellite. However, one product, solar irradiance, will no longer be produced by the second and fourth satellites.
GOES-R	Hyperspectral Environmental Suite	Measures atmospheric moisture and temperature profiles to develop weather products such as severe thunderstorm warnings and to monitor coastal regions for ecosystem health, water quality, coastal erosion, and harmful algal blooms.	This instrument was cancelled. This instrument was envisioned to provide a number of products that will be provided by another instrument. Fourteen products will not be provided. These include cloud base height, ozone layers, ocean color, turbidity, and cloud imagery.

Sources: GAO analysis of NOAA, NASA, and DOD data.

Since June 2006, the agencies have taken steps to restore selected capabilities that were removed from NPOESS in the near-term; however, they do not yet have plans to restore capabilities for the full length of time covered by the NPOESS program. Specifically, the agencies decided to restore the capabilities of three NPOESS instruments through 2016 or

2021, the capabilities of a fourth instrument through 2018 for NOAA and through 2025 for the Navy, and to accept degraded capabilities in replacing a fifth instrument between 2019 and 2024.[14] The agencies have not yet made any plans to restore the capabilities of a sixth NPOESS instrument, and NOAA has not yet made plans to restore the capabilities of the GOES-R instrument. This leaves gaps in promised capabilities ranging from 1 to 11 years, depending on the instrument. Figure 8 provides a visual summary of plans and gaps in plans for key instruments through 2026.

---

[14]The program restored the Ozone Mapping and Profiler Suite (limb) to NPP; a Total Solar Irradiance Sensor to the first NPOESS satellite; and the Clouds and the Earth's Radiant Energy System sensor (replacing the Earth Radiation Budget Sensor) to NPP and the first NPOESS satellite. In addition, both NOAA and the Navy have taken steps to procure radar altimetry sensors to be included on other satellites. The Space Environment Monitor replaces 5 of the 13 space weather products that were to be provided by the Space Environmental Sensor Suite.

Figure 8: Current Plans and Potential Gaps in Coverage for Instruments Removed from NPOESS and GOES-R

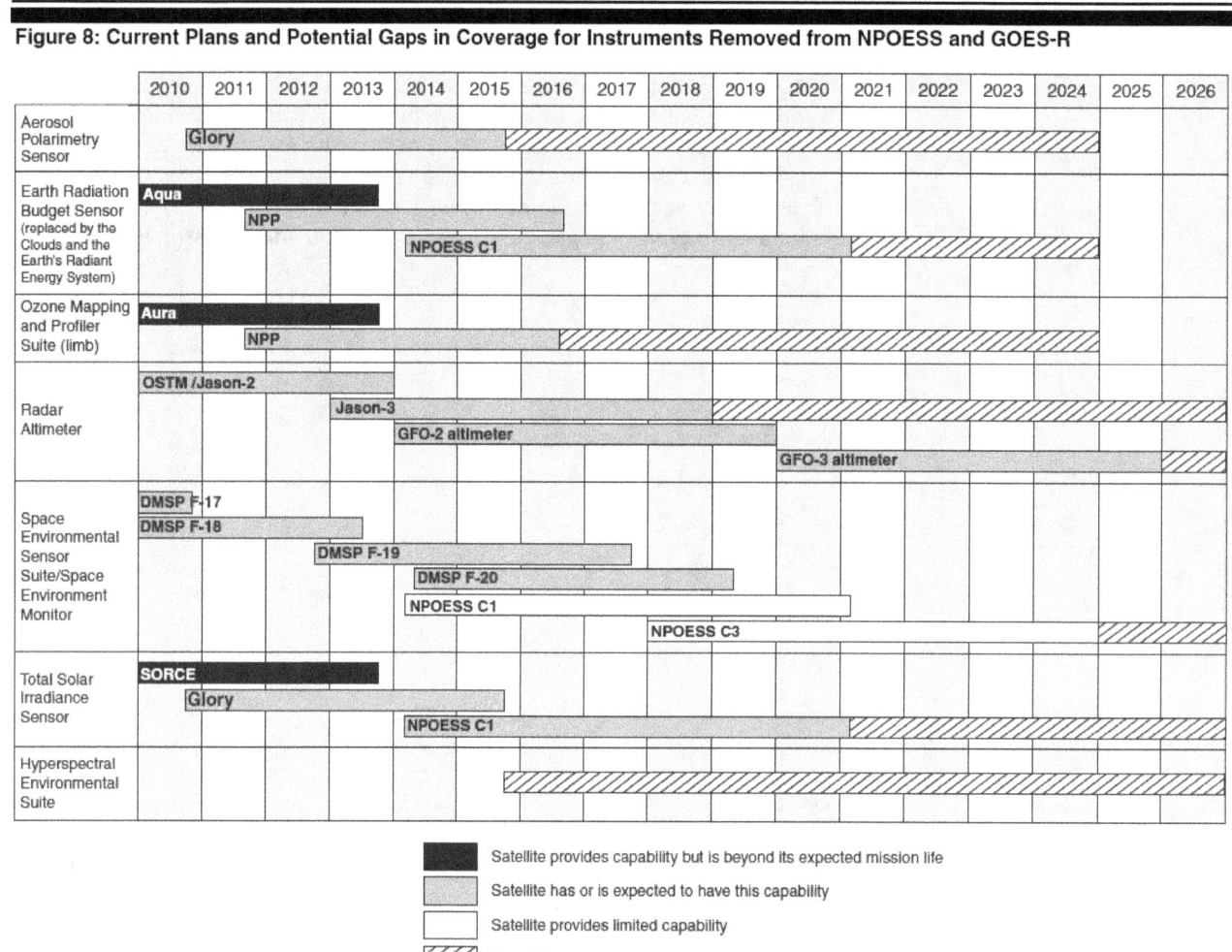

Satellite provides capability but is beyond its expected mission life

Satellite has or is expected to have this capability

Satellite provides limited capability

Capability gap

Sources: GAO analysis of DOD, NOAA, and NASA information.

Notes: The Aqua, Aura, Glory, Ocean Surface Topography Mission (OSTM)/Jason-2, and the Solar Radiation and Climate Experiment (SORCE) satellites are part of NASA's Earth Observing System mission. The Geodectic/Geophysical Satellite Follow-On (GFO) missions (GFO-2 and GFO-3) are Navy satellites. Jason-3 is a NOAA satellite.

The Conical-Scanning Microwave Imager/Sounder is not included in this chart because NOAA, NASA and DOD agreed to include a less complex sensor on the second, third, and fourth NPOESS satellites, ensuring coverage through 2026.

Both DOD and NOAA officials reiterated their commitment to look for opportunities to restore the capabilities that were removed from NPOESS and GOES-R. However, agency officials acknowledge that they do not have plans to restore the full set of capabilities because of the complexity and cost of developing new satellite programs.

Until the capabilities that were removed from NPOESS and GOES-R are restored, there will be future gaps in key atmospheric measurements, including aerosols and key cloud properties. There will also be future gaps in oceanic measurements, including sea surface height and wave height. These gaps will reduce the accuracy of key climate and space weather products—and could lead to interruptions in the continuity of data needed for accurate climate observations over time. Meteorologists, oceanographers, and climatologists reported that these gaps will seriously impact ongoing and planned earth monitoring activities.

Federal Efforts to Ensure the Long-term Provision of Satellite Climate Data Are Insufficient

For over a decade, the climate community has clamored for an interagency strategy to coordinate agency priorities, budgets, and schedules for environmental satellites over the long term—and the governance structure to implement that strategy. Specifically, in 1999, the National Research Council reported on the need for a comprehensive long-term earth observation strategy and, in 2000, for an effective governance structure that would balance interagency issues and provide authority and accountability for implementing the strategy.[15] The National Research Council has repeated these concerns in multiple reports since then.[16] Similarly, in 1999, the Administrators of NOAA and NASA wrote letters to the White House's OSTP noting the need for an interagency strategy and

---

[15]National Research Council, Climate Research Committee, *Adequacy of Climate Observing Systems* (Washington, D.C.: 1999); National Research Council, Space Studies Board: Committee on Earth Studies, *Issues in the Integration of Research and Operational Satellite Systems for Climate Research: Part I. Science and Design* (Washington, D.C.: 2000).

[16]For example, see: National Research Council, Committee on a Strategy to Mitigate the Impact of Sensor Descopes and Demanifests on the NPOESS and GOES-R Spacecraft, *Ensuring the Climate Record from the NPOESS and GOES-R Spacecraft: Elements of a Strategy to Recover Measurement Capabilities Lost in Program Restructuring,* (Washington, D.C.: 2008); National Research Council, Committee on Earth Science and Applications from Space: A Community Assessment and Strategy for the Future, *Earth Science and Applications from Space: National Imperatives for the Next Decade and Beyond* (Washington, D.C.: 2007); National Research Council, Board on Atmospheric Sciences and Climate, *From Research to Operations in Weather Satellites and Numerical Weather Prediction: Crossing the Valley of Death* (Washington, D.C.: 2000).

the means to implement it. They called for OSTP to work with OMB to better define agency roles and responsibilities and to align a satellite strategy with agency budgets. More recently, in 2008, a strategic policy research center recommended that the United States develop an overall plan for an integrated, comprehensive, and sustained earth observation system and the governance structure to support it.[17]

While progress has been made in developing near-term interagency plans, this initiative is languishing without a firm completion date, and federal efforts to establish and implement a strategy for the long-term provision of satellite data are insufficient. Specifically, in 2005, the National Science and Technology Council's Committee on Environment and Natural Resources established USGEO to develop an earth observation strategy and coordinate its implementation.[18] Since that time, USGEO assessed current and evolving requirements, evaluated them to determine investment priorities, and drafted the Strategic Assessment Report—a report delineating near-term opportunities and priorities for earth observation from both space and ground.[19] According to agency officials, this report is the first in a planned series, and it was approved by OSTP and multiple federal agencies in May 2009. However, OSTP has not yet forwarded the draft to the Committee on Environment and Natural Resources and the President's National Science and Technology Council because it is reconsidering whether to revise or move forward with the plan. USGEO officials could not provide a schedule for completing this near-term interagency plan.

This draft report is an important first step in developing a national strategy for earth observations, but it is not sufficient to ensure the long-term provision of data vital to understanding the climate. The draft report integrates different agencies' requirements and proposes continuing or improving earth observations in 17 separate areas, using both satellite and land-based measuring systems. However, the report does not include

[17]Center for Strategic and International Studies (Wigbels, Lyn et.al.), *Earth Observations and Global Change: Why? Where Are We? What Next?: A Report of CSIS Space Initiatives* (Washington, D.C.: July 2008).

[18]Interagency Working Group on Earth Observations, National Science and Technology Council, Committee on Environment and Natural Resources, *Strategic Plan for the U.S. Integrated Earth-Observation System* (Washington, D.C.: 2005).

[19]USGEO, *Observing Earth's Vital Signs, USGEO Strategic Assessment of Earth Observations: Near-Term Gaps and Opportunities (Draft)* (Washington, D.C.: May 2009).

costs, schedules, or plans for the long-term provision of satellite data. For example, it does not fully address the capabilities that were removed from the NPOESS and GOES-R missions. While the report notes the importance of continuing current plans to fly the Total Solar Irradiance Sensor on the NPP satellite and the Clouds and the Earth's Radiant Energy System sensor on the NPP and first NPOESS satellites, it does not make recommendations for what to do over the long term.

In addition, the federal government lacks a clear process for implementing an interagency strategy. Key offices within the Executive Office of the President with responsibilities for environmental observations, including OSTP and the Council for Environmental Quality, have not established processes or time frames for implementing an interagency strategy— including steps for working with OMB to ensure that agencies' annual budgets are aligned with the interagency strategy. As a result, even if an interagency strategy was finalized, it is not clear how OSTP and OMB would ensure that the responsibilities identified in the interagency strategy are consistent with agency plans and are funded within agency budgets.

Agency officials cite multiple reasons for the difficulties they have encountered over the last decade in establishing a national interagency plan for long-term earth observations. One issue involves conflicting priorities between and among agencies, including disconnects between the research and operational communities and between the weather and climate communities. Another issue is the lack of agreement on how and when to transition research capabilities to operational satellites—and how to fund them.

Without a long-term interagency strategy for satellite observations, and a means for implementing it, agencies face gaps in satellite data and risk making ad hoc decisions on individual satellites. For example, until recently, NASA's QuikScat research satellite provided measurements of the effect of wind on ocean surfaces, which were used by the National Weather Service to improve tropical and midlatitude storm warnings and by the National/Naval Ice Center to improve its understanding of Arctic and Antarctic ice environments.[20] However, NOAA does not plan to replace the satellite until at least 2014. This extended gap leaves the organizations that used QuikScat with degraded measurements. As

---

[20]The main antenna on the QuikScat satellite failed in November 2009, rendering it useless to forecasters. The satellite was 8 years past its expected life span.

another example, Landsat satellites have provided data on land cover change, vegetation mapping, and wildfire effects for over 35 years.[21] Currently, there are two Landsat satellites in operation, and both are long past their expected life spans. While there is a plan to develop and launch the Landsat Data Continuity Mission by June 2013, there is no commitment to ensure continuity after that mission.[22] Without Landsat or a similar satellite program, there will be a significant gap in land cover images and other important global climate data ranging from water management to agriculture.

Until an interagency strategy for earth observation is established, and a clear process for implementing it is in place, federal agencies will continue to procure their immediate priorities on an ad hoc basis, the economic benefits of a coordinated approach to investments in earth observation may be lost, and the continuity of key measurements may be lost. This will hinder our nation's ability to understand long-term climate changes.

Federal Agencies Lack a Strategy for the Long-term Provision of Space Weather Data

While key federal agencies have taken steps to plan for continued space weather observations in the near term, they lack a strategy for the long-term provision of space weather data. Similar to maintaining satellite-provided climate observations, maintaining space weather observations over the long term is important. The National Space Weather Program, the interagency coordinating body for the United States space weather community, has repeatedly recommended taking action to sustain the space weather observation infrastructure on a long-term basis.

Agencies participating in the National Space Weather Program have taken short-term actions that may help alleviate near-term gaps in space weather observations, but OSTP has not approved or released two reports that are expected to establish plans for obtaining space weather observations over the long term. Both NOAA and DOD are seeking to replace key

---

[21]The Landsat program is jointly managed by NASA and the U.S. Geological Survey.

[22]In August 2007, a White House working group called the Future of Land Imaging Interagency Working Group issued A Plan for a U.S. National Land Imaging Program. This report recommended that the Department of the Interior manage future Landsat programs and have NASA develop future satellites. However, this plan has not yet been implemented.

experimental space-observing satellites.[23] In addition, at OSTP's request, the National Space Weather Program reported in 2008 on the impacts for both operations and research of not having NASA's aging Advanced Composition Explorer or the planned space weather capabilities from the NPOESS program. It subsequently developed, again at the request of OSTP, two reports documenting specific recommendations for the future of space weather, one on what to do about the Advanced Composition Explorer and the other on the replacement of the space weather capabilities removed from the NPOESS program. The program submitted the reports in October and November of 2009, respectively. However, OSTP officials do not have a schedule for approving or releasing the reports.

While the agencies' short-term actions and the pending reports hold promise, federal agencies do not currently have a comprehensive interagency strategy for the long-term provision of space weather data. Until OSTP releases the reports, it will not be clear whether they provide a clear strategy to ensure the long-term provision of space weather data—or whether the current efforts are simply ad hoc attempts to ensure short-term data continuity. Without a comprehensive long-term strategy for the provision of space weather data, agencies may make ad hoc decisions to ensure continuity in the near term and risk making inefficient decisions on key investments.

Conclusions

Almost 4 years after key climate and space weather instruments were removed from the NPOESS and GOES-R satellite programs, there are still significant gaps in future satellite coverage. While individual agencies have taken steps to restore selected capabilities in the near term, gaps in coverage ranging from 1 to 11 years are expected beginning as soon as 2015. The gaps in satellite coverage are expected to affect the continuity of important climate and space weather measurements, such as our understanding of how weather cycles impact global food production, and

---

[23]NOAA has requested funding in fiscal year 2011 to refurbish NASA's Deep Space Climate Observatory spacecraft to replace the experimental Advanced Composition Explorer spacecraft and has requested funding to replace its Constellation Observing System for Meteorology, Ionosphere, and Climate. DOD issued a request for information to replace its experimental Communication/Navigation Outage Forecasting System satellite, which is designed to sense space weather that affects how the Global Positioning System, high-frequency radio, and other communications devices work in low latitude areas.

when radio and GPS satellite communications are likely to be affected by space weather.

Looking more broadly, despite repeated calls for interagency strategies for the long-term provision of environmental data (both for climate and space weather purposes), our nation still lacks such plans. Efforts to develop even short-term strategies have languished in committees and offices supporting the Executive Office of the President, and there is no schedule for them to be approved or released. Further, even if an interagency strategy for the long-term provision of environmental observations was established, there are not clear processes in place to implement it or align it with individual agencies' plans and annual budgets. Specifically, key organizations within the Executive Office of the President, including the Office of Science and Technology Policy, the Office of Management and Budget, and the Council on Environmental Quality, lack a coordinated process for ensuring that individual agencies align their plans and budgets to the greater good identified in an interagency plan.

Until the Executive Office of the President establishes comprehensive interagency strategies and internal processes that foster the implementation of these strategies, individual agencies will continue to address their most pressing priorities as they arise and opportunities to effectively and efficiently plan ahead will be lost.

Recommendations for Executive Action

In order to effectively address our country's need for sustained environmental observations, we recommend that the Assistant to the President for Science and Technology, in collaboration with key Executive Office of the President entities (including the Office of Science and Technology Policy, the Office of Management and Budget, the Council on Environmental Quality, and the National Science and Technology Council), take the following four actions:

- Establish a firm deadline for the completion and release of three key reports on environmental observations:

  - USGEO's report on near-term priorities and opportunities in earth observations, called the Strategic Assessment Report;

  - The National Space Weather Program's report on how to address the loss of the Advanced Composition Explorer capabilities; and

- The National Space Weather Program's report on how to address the space weather capabilities that were removed from the NPOESS program.

- Direct USGEO to establish an interagency strategy to address the long-term provision of environmental observations from satellites that includes costs and schedules for the satellites, as well as a plan for the relevant agencies' future budgets.

- Establish an ongoing process, with timelines, for obtaining approval of the interagency strategy and aligning it with agency plans and annual budgets.

- Direct the National Space Weather Program Council to establish an interagency strategy for the long-term provision of space weather observations.

Agency Comments and Our Evaluation

A senior policy analyst from the Office of Science and Technology Policy/Executive Office of the President provided comments on a draft of this report via e-mail. In addition, we received written comments on a draft of this report from the Secretary of Commerce, who transmitted NOAA's comments (see app. IV), and NASA's Associate Administrator for its Science Mission Directorate (see app. V). DOD officials declined to comment on a draft of the report.

The Executive Office of the President did not agree or disagree with our recommendations; however, officials noted that OSTP is currently revising USGEO's Strategic Assessment Report to update information on launch schedules and on the availability of certain measurements that have changed since completion of the report a year ago. Further, officials agreed that the Strategic Assessment Report is a first step in developing a strategy for earth observations, and noted that they plan to use the report as a basis for meeting congressional reporting requirements directing OSTP to develop a strategy on earth observations. In crafting this strategy, it will be important for OSTP to address long-term interagency needs and to work with OMB to ensure that the long-term plans are aligned with individual agencies' plans and budgets. If the plan does not include these elements, individual agencies will continue to address only their most pressing priorities, other agencies' needs may be ignored, and the government may lose the ability to effectively and efficiently address its earth observation needs.

In its comments, NOAA noted that it had completed its actions relative to delivering input to the Executive Office of the President for developing strategies for climate and space weather observations. We agree; it is now up to the Executive Office of the President to establish and implement an interagency strategy for the long-term provision of these observations. The agency also responded to our statement that it had not established plans to restore all of the capabilities that were removed from the GOES-R and NPOESS programs. Regarding GOES-R, NOAA stated that it will continue to evaluate the feasibility and priority of addressing requirements and determine the appropriate means to meet them.

Regarding NPOESS, NOAA noted that, in fiscal year 2009, the agency restored the highest priority climate sensors that were removed from the NPOESS program. NOAA also reported that the fiscal year 2011 President's Budget Request includes plans to restore additional key climate sensors on JPSS and other satellite programs. However, as discussed in our report, NOAA's efforts to restore sensors in 2009 addressed only selected near-term needs and did not address the full set of capabilities over the life of the NPOESS program. Further, regarding the fiscal year 2011 President's Budget Request, at the time of our review the full set of capabilities planned for the JPSS program had not yet been determined. For example, the Total Solar Irradiance Sensor (which was one of the high-priority sensors that was restored to the NPOESS program in fiscal year 2009) will not be included on the JPSS satellite, but could instead be included on another to-be-determined satellite. As noted several times in our report, we focused on the capabilities that were planned for the NPOESS program because plans for JPSS had not yet been finalized. We have ongoing work to examine the JPSS program, which will further evaluate NOAA's plans as they are solidified. In a final comment, NOAA stated that we did not distinguish between potential data gaps in existing and new capabilities, and suggested that we only use the term "gap" to describe the potential loss of an existing capability. Given that the requirements for the NPOESS programs were developed and validated by multiple agencies nearly a decade ago, and requirements for the GOES-R sensor were revalidated by NOAA in 2007, we believe it is appropriate to view the removal of these requirements as gaps—whether they represent existing or new capabilities.

In its written comments, NASA provided further details on its efforts to advance the understanding of earth systems and Heliophysics through environmental research satellites, and provided clarification on plans for future missions that are included in the fiscal year 2011 President's Budget Request. The agency also noted that OSTP developed a plan for the future of the land-imaging program, under which NASA would develop future Landsat-like satellites on behalf of the Department of the Interior. However, this plan was established in 2007 and has not yet been funded or implemented. It is not clear that it will be implemented. This situation illustrates that having an approved plan is not enough to ensure that critical satellite capabilities are obtained, and reiterates the need for an ongoing process that aligns interagency strategies with individual agencies' plans and annual budgets.

OSTP, NOAA, and NASA also provided technical comments on the report, which we incorporated as appropriate.

As agreed with your offices, unless you publicly announce the contents of this report earlier, we plan no further distribution until 30 days from the report date. At that time, we will send copies of this report to interested congressional committees, the Secretary of Commerce, the Secretary of Defense, the Administrator of NASA, the Director of the Office of Science and Technology Policy, the Director of the Office of Management and Budget, and other interested parties. The report also will be available on the GAO Web site at http://www.gao.gov.

If you or your staff members have questions about this report, please contact me at (202) 512-9286 or pownerd@gao.gov. Contact points for our Offices of Congressional Relations and Public Affairs may be found on the last page of this report. GAO staff who made key contributions to this report are listed in appendix VI.

David A. Powner
Director, Information Technology Management Issues

Appendix I: Objectives, Scope, and Methodology

Our objectives were to (1) assess plans to restore capabilities that were originally planned for, but then removed from, the National Polar-orbiting Operational Environmental Satellite System (NPOESS) and Geostationary Operational Environmental Satellite-R series (GOES-R) satellites; (2) evaluate the adequacy of federal efforts to establish a strategy for the long-term provision of satellite-provided climate data; and (3) evaluate the adequacy of federal efforts to establish a strategy for the long-term provision of satellite-provided space weather data. To assess plans for restoring capabilities from the NPOESS and GOES-R programs, we compared the original program plans for sensors and products with current plans and identified gaps over time. We also observed monthly senior-level management review meetings, reviewed documentation from those meetings, and interviewed agency officials to obtain information on any changes in program plans.

To evaluate the adequacy of federal efforts to establish a strategy for the long-term provision of satellite-provided climate data, we compared plans developed by the Department of Defense (DOD), National Aeronautics and Space Administration (NASA), National Oceanic and Atmospheric Administration (NOAA), and a draft strategy developed by the Executive Office of the President's Office of Science and Technology Policy (OSTP) and the U.S. Group on Earth Observations for the provision of climate data with recommendations made by the National Research Council and GAO for the development of a long-term strategy. We identified the shortfalls of and challenges to those plans. We also visited NOAA's National Climatic Data Center, Climate Prediction Center, and Earth System Research Laboratory; the Navy's Fleet Numerical Meteorology and Oceanography Center and Naval Oceanographic Office; and the Air Force Weather Agency to obtain information on the uses and users of satellite data for climate monitoring and prediction, as well the need for interagency strategic planning for space-based climate observations. We also interviewed relevant agency officials.

To evaluate the adequacy of federal efforts to establish a strategy for the long-term provision of satellite-provided space weather data, we compared DOD, NASA, and NOAA plans for the provision of space weather data to leading practices for the development of a long-term strategy, and we identified the potential shortfalls of and challenges to those plans. We also identified OSTP plans for space weather. We attended a space weather events workshop to determine key issues related to long-term plans for space weather observations. We also visited the Air Force Weather Agency, the Space Weather Prediction Center, and NOAA's National Geophysical Data Center to obtain information on the uses and users of satellite data for space weather monitoring and prediction, as well the need for interagency strategic planning for space weather observations. We also interviewed relevant agency officials.

We conducted our work at NOAA, NASA, DOD, and OSTP facilities in the Washington, D.C., metropolitan area. In addition, we conducted work at satellite data processing facilities in Asheville, North Carolina; Monterey, California; Boulder, Colorado; Bay Saint Louis, Mississippi; and Omaha, Nebraska. We selected these facilities because they host key military and civilian users of satellite data for weather, climate, and space weather forecasting. We conducted this performance audit from June 2009 to April 2010, in accordance with generally accepted government auditing standards. Those standards require that we plan and perform the audit to obtain sufficient, appropriate evidence to provide a reasonable basis for our findings and conclusions based on our audit objectives. We believe that the evidence obtained provides a reasonable basis for our findings and conclusions based on our audit objectives.

Appendix II: Key Federal Organizations with Climate and Space Weather Responsibilities

Multiple agencies have a role in developing or using climate and space weather products. Table 5 lists key federal organizations' roles with respect to climate observation, while table 6 lists key federal organizations' roles with respect to space weather observation.

Table 5: Key Federal Organizations' Roles for Climate Observation

Federal agency/organization	Role/responsibility
Department of Agriculture	Monitors environmental conditions and exploits environmental observations and land remote sensing to map and monitor the health, quality, and production of US and global crop conditions for many applications including commodity price stabilization and food security. Environmental observations are used to aid in making payments to producers and as an input for monitoring program integrity for farm, conservation, and insurance programs. Environmental conditions are used as an input to monitoring forest health, wildland fire fuels, and fire behavior.
Department of Commerce/ National Oceanic and Atmospheric Administration	Monitors and predicts changes in the earth's environment and oceans and acquires and operates environmental satellites, including polar-orbiting and geostationary environmental satellites; also has multiple subagencies with responsibilities for using this satellite data to develop weather and climate products; manages the Polar Operational Environmental Satellite and Geostationary Operational Environmental Satellite programs, which provide environmental data used for developing graphical weather images and specialized weather products, forecasting weather through numerical weather prediction models and monitoring other environmental phenomena.
National Environmental Satellite, Data, and Information Service	Manages the development and operations of satellites and remote-based observations; its National Climatic Data Center stores and disseminates climate data observed through satellites and makes them accessible to the nation and public.
National Weather Service	Provides weather and climate forecasts for the protection of life and property and the enhancement of the national economy. One of several National Centers for Environmental Prediction within the National Weather Service, the Climate Prediction Center provides products and services that describe, assess, monitor, and predict (e.g., forecasts/outlooks ranging from days to seasons to years) the earth's environment.
Office of Oceanic and Atmospheric Research	Conducts analytical and theoretical climate research experiments to better understand and predict climate variability and change and to enhance society's ability to plan and respond to global change; includes labs, like the Earth System Research Laboratory, which conduct research to develop new or improved products/services and models.
Department of Commerce/ National Institute of Standards and Technology	Provides measurements and standards that support accurate and reliable climate observations; also performs calibrations and special tests of a wide range of instruments and techniques for accurate measurements.
Department of Defense	Manages the defense polar-orbiting operational satellite program, called the Defense Meteorological Satellite Program, which provides environmental data used for developing graphical weather images and specialized weather products, forecasting weather through numerical weather prediction models, and monitoring other environmental phenomena.

Federal agency/organization	Role/responsibility
U.S. Navy	Monitors environmental conditions that may impact military operations in the oceans and near coastal communities; its Fleet Numerical Meteorology and Oceanography Center monitors atmospheric and oceanographic data to provide tailored global weather forecasts and analyses on environmental conditions ranging from days to several months in advance that may affect Navy, Marine Corps, and other military planning and operations; its Naval Oceanographic Office analyzes oceanographic and hydrographic data to develop products that detail environmental conditions (e.g., acoustics and physics) from the ocean's floor to its surface.
Air Force Weather Agency	Monitors environmental conditions that may impact military operations on land, in the air, and in space; collects, analyzes, and predicts environmental information to provide tailored regional and global weather forecasts and effects caused by environmental conditions ranging from hours to several months in advance that may affect Air Force, Army, Special Operations, and intelligence community planning and operations.
Department of Energy	Conducts climate research in order to understand how energy production and use (e.g., changes in greenhouse gas and aerosol concentrations) may impact the global climate system. Develops models that simulate the effects of climate change and uses field and laboratory observations to interpret and extend the results of such model simulations.
Department of Health and Human Services	Uses satellite observations to conduct research related to environmental health and the health effects of climate changes, including effects of ultraviolet radiation/exposure (skin, eyes, immune system) and emerging infectious diseases.
Department of Homeland Security/ Federal Emergency Management Agency	Uses climate research and predictions to develop disaster preparedness and response plans.
Department of the Interior/ U.S. Geological Survey	Focuses on understanding past and present climate and their effects on landscapes, land cover and use, and ecosystems. Manages the Landsat satellite programs in conjunction with the National Aeronautics and Space Administration.
Department of State	Contributes to and participates in international coordination bodies, such as the United Nations Framework Convention on Climate Change and the Intergovernmental Panel on Climate Change, which use U.S. climate assessments as the basis of certain findings in their international climate assessments, and helps facilitate federal agency coordination with international climate research efforts.
Department of Transportation	Conducts climate research to (1) examine the potential impacts of climate variability and change on transportation infrastructure and services; (2) increase energy efficiency and reduce greenhouse gases; and (3) improve transportation-related greenhouse gas data and modeling.
Environmental Protection Agency	Assesses the impacts of climate variability and change on air quality, water quality, aquatic ecosystems, and human health. From these assessments, it develops options for adaptation to be considered by decision makers.
National Aeronautics and Space Administration/Earth Science Division	Operates research satellites under the Earth Observing System program. Many of these satellites provide climate observations used by a variety of federal agencies, universities, and nongovernmental organizations. The agency's climate mission is to advance the state of science of the global integrated earth system, including interactions among the global and regional atmosphere, oceans, sea ice, lands, and ecosystems.
National Science Foundation	Educates the public and funds research to advance the state of science, including understanding climate elements such as physical, chemical, biological, and human systems and the interactions among them.

Federal agency/organization	Role/responsibility
Smithsonian Institution	Conducts research of atmospheric processes, ecosystem dynamics, natural and anthropogenic environmental change, and historical museum records/artifacts, as well as geologic records; its research is intended to have a long-term (i.e., decadal) perspective.
U.S. Agency for International Development	Uses satellite observations to provide U.S. and foreign decision makers—both in the United States and in the developing world—with information designed to support policy and program interventions for effective and timely response to drought and food insecurity.

Sources: GAO analysis of agency information from DOD, NASA, NOAA, the U.S. Group on Earth Observations (USGEO), and the U.S. Global Change Research Program (USGCRP).

Table 6: Key Federal Organizations' Roles for Space Weather Observation

Federal agency/organization	Role/responsibility
Department of Commerce/ National Oceanic and Atmospheric Administration	Monitors the space weather environment and provides operational forecasts, warnings, and alerts. Within the National Oceanic and Atmospheric Administration, the National Weather Service is responsible for providing weather forecasts for the protection of life and property and the enhancement of the national economy. Its Space Weather Prediction Center provides forecasts and warnings of space weather events that may impact space-based assets such as Global Positioning System (GPS) satellites, and earth-based assets such as the energy grid.
Department of Defense	Conducts space weather monitoring through the Air Force to mitigate and minimize adverse space weather impacts on operational readiness, mission operations, and military capabilities, as well as to provide military planners with space situational awareness.
Department of Energy	Uses observations from space weather satellites to detect nuclear events; in addition, it uses space weather data to examine possible impacts on electrical energy transmission (i.e., the energy grid).
Department of the Interior	Provides ground-based magnetometer data continuously from 14 observatories distributed across the United States and its territories through the U.S. Geological Survey; collects, transports, and disseminates these data for global-scale monitoring of the earth's magnetic field, which can be affected by space weather.
Department of State	The Department of State's Office of Space and Advanced Technology (OES/SAT) ensures that U.S. space policies and multilateral science activities, including space weather, support U.S. foreign policy objectives and enhance U.S. space and technological competitiveness. OES/SAT has primary responsibility for U.S. representation to the United Nations' Committee on the Peaceful Uses of Outer Space. The office also leads interagency coordination on all civil space-related international agreements and plays a key role in the implementation of National Space Policy focused on dual-use space applications such as space-based positioning, navigation, and timing, satellite-based remote sensing and earth observation, and space weather monitoring.
Department of Transportation	Examines space weather impacts to navigation (e.g., GPS) and radiation exposure at high altitudes; its Federal Aviation Administration considers space weather impacts in optimizing national and international aviation weather systems and services.
National Aeronautics and Space Administration	Develops and manages satellite operations that contribute to space weather observations; conducts research of the solar-terrestrial system to improve and advance our understanding of events and conditions in space and to develop and use new technology; explores how solar activity may potentially impact humans in space, as well as space-based assets such as solar research satellites like the Advanced Composition Explorer and Solar and Heliospheric Observatory and robotic assets that explore characteristics of other planets.
National Science Foundation	Conducts research to increase fundamental understanding of space environment processes and to improve space weather predictive capabilities.

Source: GAO analysis of agency information from the National Space Weather Program, Air Force Weather Agency, and Space Weather Prediction Center.

Appendix III: Federal Organizations That Participate in Interagency Coordination Groups

Interagency committees coordinate the interests of the multiple federal agencies whose missions involve environmental monitoring and research. These include the U.S. Global Change Research Program, which coordinates federal climate research efforts; the U.S. Group on Earth Observations, which plans for and coordinates earth observations; and the National Space Weather Program, which coordinates federal space weather monitoring, research, and forecasts. Table 7 identifies federal organizations that participate in these interagency coordination groups.

Table 7: Federal Organizations That Participate in Interagency Coordination Groups

Federal organizations	U.S. Group on Earth Observations	U.S. Global Change Research Program	National Space Weather Program
Agencies			
Department of Agriculture	X	X	
Department of Commerce	X	X	X
Department of Defense	X	X	X
Department of Energy	X	X	X
Department of Health and Human Services	X	X	
Department of Homeland Security	X		X[a]
Department of the Interior	X	X	X
Department of State	X	X	X
Department of Transportation	X	X	X
Environmental Protection Agency	X	X	
National Aeronautics and Space Administration	X	X	X
National Science Foundation	X	X	X
Smithsonian Institution	X	X	
U.S. Agency for International Development	X	X	
Executive Office of the President			
Council on Environmental Quality		X	
Office of Management and Budget	X	X	X
Office of Science and Technology Policy	X	X	X

Source: GAO based on interagency group documents.

[a]Agency officials noted that they are working with Homeland Security's Federal Emergency Management Agency to have it participate in the National Space Weather Program.

Appendix IV: Comments from the Department of Commerce

UNITED STATES DEPARTMENT OF COMMERCE
The Secretary of Commerce
Washington, D.C. 20230

April 9, 2010

Mr. David A. Powner
Director
Information Technology Management Issues
U.S. Government Accountability Office
441 G Street, NW
Washington, DC 20548

Dear Mr. Powner:

     Thank you for the opportunity to review and comment on the Government Accountability Office's draft report entitled "Environmental Satellites: Strategy Needed to Sustain Critical Climate and Space Weather Measurements" (GAO-10-456). On behalf of the Department of Commerce, I have enclosed the National Oceanic and Atmospheric Administration's comments on the draft report.

               Sincerely,

               Gary Locke

Enclosure

Department of Commerce
National Oceanic and Atmospheric Administration
Comments to the Draft GAO Report Entitled
"Environmental Satellites: Strategy Needed to Sustain
Critical Climate and Space Weather Measurements"
(GAO-10-456, April 2010)

<u>General Comments</u>

The Department of Commerce and the National Oceanic and Atmospheric Administration
(NOAA) appreciate the opportunity to review this report on environmental satellites. The report
describes four ongoing activities at the NOAA National Environmental Satellite, Data, and
Information Service: (a) the full set of National Polar-orbiting Operational Environmental
Satellite System (NPOESS) capabilities removed in 2006; (b) advanced climate capabilities for
Geostationary Orbiting Environmental Satellite, Series R (GOES-R) removed in 2006; (c) a
report submitted to the Executive Office of the President, which identifies and prioritizes near-
term opportunities for environmental observations; and (d) two reports submitted to the White
House's Office of Science and Technology Policy on how to mitigate the loss of key satellites
and instruments.

The report accurately describes the status of items (c) and (d), as listed above. Our actions are
complete. For item (a), the report states that NOAA has not established plans for recovering
capabilities lost when NPOESS was restructured in 2006. NOAA does have a plan to restore
capabilities for the climate sensors, which was implemented in fiscal year (FY) 2009, when
NOAA began funding the National Aeronautics and Space Administration's (NASA) instrument
development projects to restore the highest priority climate sensors that were removed from
NPOESS in 2006. The FY 2011 President's budget request includes a plan for NOAA to
continue restoring key climate sensors removed from NPOESS and host the climate sensors on a
NOAA satellite program called the Joint Polar Satellite System (JPSS). Also included in the
FY 2011 request is a plan to complete the development of the Jason 3 satellite with NASA and
our European partners and plan for a continuity altimetry mission after Jason 3.

For item (b), the report states that NOAA has not made any plans to restore the advanced climate
capabilities of the instrument that was removed from GOES-R. The referenced instrument is the
Hyperspectral Environmental Suite (HES), an instrument concept for measuring high-resolution
vertical profiles of temperature and water vapor and providing images of the coastal ocean.
Early GOES-R instrument concept studies proved that the HES concept was too technically
advanced to be accommodated on the GOES-R spacecraft. NOAA will continue to evaluate the
feasibility and priority of addressing HES requirements and determine the most appropriate
methods to meet them.

In general, the report does not differentiate between gaps in existing operational observation and
delays, potential or real, in bringing new observations into operational use. We would suggest
that the term "gap" only be utilized to describe potential loss of an existing operational capability
or established climate record.

Appendix V: Comments from the National Aeronautics and Space Administration

Mr. David A. Powner
Director, Information Technology Management Issues
U.S. Government Accountability Office
Washington, DC 20548

Dear Mr. Powner:

NASA appreciates the opportunity to comment on your draft report entitled, "Environmental Satellites: Strategy Needed to Sustain Critical Climate and Space Weather Measurements," (GAO-10-456).

While no recommendations in the report were directed to NASA, the report contains several points that require clarification.

NASA's Earth Science Division, as described on Page 20, is responsible for advancing the understanding of the Earth system and the science and technology of remote sensing through its environmental research satellites. NASA makes new measurements and creates new technologies for measuring climate through various satellite and airborne missions, including the Earth Observing System. With these new measurements, NASA uncovers the mechanics and interrelationships of Earth system processes, creates climate data records that can be extended by subsequent research or operational satellites, and pioneers the use of new observations in climate models to improve their assessment and predictive capabilities. NASA's Heliophysics Division, as described on Page 21, conducts space weather research and development activities using research satellites. Data from these satellites are used for Heliophysics research and are also provided to other agencies for operational space weather forecasting.

With regards to future research satellites, as detailed on Page 11, NASA's Earth Science Division currently has five "foundational" missions (Glory, Aquarius, NPOESS Preparatory Project, Landsat Data Continuity Mission (LDCM), and Global Precipitation Measurement) scheduled for launch between 2010 and 2013. The Fiscal Year (FY) 2011 President's Budget Request includes funding for a replacement to the Orbiting Carbon Observatory, to launch in February 2013. Of the missions recommended by the National Research Council in its 2007 Decadal Survey, "Earth Science and Applications from Space: National Imperatives for the Next Decade and Beyond," the FY2011 Budget Request funds all Tier 1 missions to be launched in the three-year period from late 2014 to late 2017, achieving the scientific synergies intended by the Decadal Survey for those

missions. Tier 2 missions are also accelerated by the Budget Request, with two to be
launched by the end of 2020.

With regard to the Landsat family of satellites described on Page 20, the Landsat program
is a joint effort between NASA and the U.S. Geological Survey (USGS). NASA
develops and launches the Landsat satellites, while USGS is responsible for operating the
satellites and distributing and archiving the data. The next Landsat mission, LDCM, is
currently scheduled for launch between December 2012 and June 2013. With regards to
the future of the Landsat program, as discussed on Page 32, in 2007, the Office of
Science and Technology Policy issued a plan for a Department of the Interior-led U.S.
National Land Imaging Program to acquire Landsat-type data beyond LDCM, but that
plan has not yet been implemented. Under this construct, future Landsat-type satellites
would be developed by NASA on a reimbursable basis, much like the civil weather
satellites.

Thank you again for the opportunity to review and comment on this draft report. We
look forward to your final report to Congress.

Sincerely,

Edward J. Weiler
Associate Administrator for
Science Mission Directorate

Appendix VI: GAO Contact and Staff Acknowledgments

GAO Contact	David A. Powner, (202) 512-9286, or pownerd@gao.gov
Staff Acknowledgments	In addition to the individual named above, Colleen M. Phillips, Assistant Director; Bill Carrigg; Neil Doherty; Joshua Leiling; Kathleen S. Lovett; Lee McCracken; and Joseph D. Thompson made key contributions to this report.

www.ingramcontent.com/pod-product-compliance
Lightning Source LLC
Chambersburg PA
CBHW060531010626
45794CB00023B/3308